HOME

HOME

What It Means and
Why It Matters

Mary Gordon

STERLING

New York / London
www.sterlingpublishing.com

STERLING and the distinctive Sterling logo are registered
trademarks of Sterling Publishing Co., Inc.

Library of Congress Cataloging-in-Publication Data Available

10 9 8 7 6 5 4 3 2 1

Published by Sterling Publishing Co., Inc.
387 Park Avenue South, New York, N.Y. 10016
Copyright © 2010 Mary Gordon
Distributed in Canada by Sterling Publishing
c/o Canadian Manda Group, 165 Dufferin Street
Toronto, Ontario, Canada M6K 3H6
Distributed in the United Kingdom by GMC Distribution Services
Castle Place, 166 High Street, Lewes, East Sussex, England BN7 1XU
Distributed in Australia by Capricorn Link (Australia) Pty. Ltd.
P.O. Box 704, Windsor, NSW 2756, Australia

Sterling ISBN 978-1-4027-6836-1

For information about custom editions, special sales,
premium and corporate purchases, please contact
Sterling Special Sales Department at 800-805-5489
or specialsales@sterlingpublishing.com.

FOR MEREDITH AND JOSH

CONTENTS

Home is a name, a word,
it is a strong one; stronger
than magician ever spoke,
or spirit ever answered to,
in the strongest conjuration.

—Charles Dickens

one

What Makes a House a Home?

A man to whom I was briefly married said to me one day, toward the end of our time together, "You don't deserve to live in a house." For a terrible moment I believed him. He thought he was making a point about my untidiness; I understood it as proof of the impossibility of a shared life. We were both right; because "house" is a word that sounds simple; it's one of the first a child learns; the image is one of the first a child learns to draw. And yet what happens in a house is simply: life. And what could be less simple than that.

"Food, clothing, and shelter," the minimum required to sustain a life. Of the three, shelter is the one requiring the greatest investment of resources, and it is the one whose connection to time is strongest and most real. A meal literally decomposes within hours; a dress still fashionable in a decade earns the term "classic." But the places where we live: we expect them to outlive us. They are built with an eye to the future . . . and, of course, the past, both real and fantasized.

We live in houses—why? Not just to keep us from the elements. Survival is only one part of what we do with where we live. We inhabit spaces so that we can be safe to be who we are, so that we are out of the public eye, so that what we treasure is protected, cared for, showcased. We *live* at home, whether it is a yurt or a skyscraper. We sleep, entertain friends, rear our children, read, listen to music. We work where we live or we escape from work to go there. Our homes are also about display: how much we are worth, what our taste is. They are the source of our wealth and they drain it. They allow us repose and they demand what sometimes seems to be endless attention. For many women, the house is a metaphor for the body: and all important life is lived within its walls. And what is it to be without one? To be homeless is to be outside the web of the civilized.

"Where do you live?" This would seem to be a simple question, easily answerable, as the idea of a house would seem simple and almost automatically accessible. But it is, in reality, a complicated question. What is required to provide a proper answer is a thorough consideration of two words in the question: *where* and *live*.

In his strange, alternately fascinating and maddening meditation, *The Poetics of Space,* the late French philosopher Gaston Bachelard asks: "Where is the main stress, for instance, in *being there*, on *being*, or on *there*?"[1] In that vein, we might ask the question, What do we mean by live? What do we mean by where?

As I write this, I am living in what could be called a house, but it has very little in common with anything a seventeenth-century Dutchman would have called by that name. It is not really a house; it is a part of what is called a housing complex, and it is very different from anywhere I have ever lived. It is not, I think, a good place to be living: I will only live here for some weeks . . . and so I make of it what I must. But the differences between it and other places I have lived, places I think of as good places to be living,

. . . home to people like me is not a place but all places, all places except the one we happen to be in at the moment.

—Anthony Burgess

make real to me some of the important questions that surround our habit of habitation.

My unease here isn't because I'm not living in a single-family dwelling. I have been very happy in places that were not houses, but apartments. I have even been quite blissfully happy in hotels. And so I try to pinpoint what is not here, what other happy places have given me.

I will live here for three months, a quarter of a year. It is, in many ways, a sensible thing to be doing; I am quite near the university where I will be teaching and one of a renter's problems isn't a problem here: dogs are allowed, and I have two and they are entirely necessary for my mental health. So I am grateful to have a place to lay my head and their paws.

The day after I move in, I am called to the central office, to sign a lease. The lease is twenty-four pages long. Two pages for every week I will live here. Of course I do not read the pages that I sign, or initial, twenty-four times, at the bottom of every page. I swear to pay for whatever I damage; I waive insurance, because I can't imagine that anything here is damageable, or valuable. Nothing here seems precious or irreplaceable: it occurs to me that this may be connected to everything being "trouble free."

The representative of the management company assures me that living here will be "trouble free." He gives me a key to the gym, the outdoor heated swimming pool, the hot tub. He tells me the rules about garbage. He tells me that hot coffee is available to me in the office, five days a week, eight A.M. to five P.M. He gives me the schedule for the free shuttle that will take me to the campus where I will be working: it will come every half hour. It does not come after eight thirty P.M. or on weekends. He hopes that everything will "work for me" and suggests (or do I imagine this?) that if it doesn't, it will be my fault.

Today, for the third time, I put my key in the wrong door: I tried to open apartment 156 instead of 256. I was grateful no one was home any of the three times, so I didn't have to confess to my failure of attentiveness. Of course, if I had for some reason opened the door, I would have known instantly I was not "at home." Because although the little house-lets are identically constructed, we have placed things inside them that mark them as ours.

I am oddly reluctant to buy things that will mark the place as mine—I understand that this is quite unlike me. The last time I lived somewhere for a few months, I brought with me paintings, dishes, linens, vases, rugs. Partly this was a practical matter: my temporary dwelling was only four hours from my permanent home, and I could make several trips, bring things in stages. Whereas this new dwelling is three thousand miles from my home; there is no going back and forth, no time for frivolous mistakes that could be easily amended. But partly my decision is because this place makes me feel hopeless: it is white and square and new; the carpets are oatmeal-colored, and this provides the most vivid tone in the place. I have been provided with what was called a "minimum start-up hospitality packet": white towels, white sheets, an oatmeal-colored blanket made largely, I think, of petroleum, a two-tone brown comforter that is usually too warm, except when it isn't warm enough. So why don't I just throw caution to the winds, put the hospitality packet in its box in the closet, spend several hundred dollars on bedding, give it away, if necessary, to some grateful and surprised unfortunates who'd have a particularly good day at the Salvation Army?

It is because this place has for me stamped out entirely the possibility of the personal. And because, unlike my other temporary dwelling, which looked out on a wonderful old maple that shed its leaves and put out new ones: first insouciantly yellow-green, then taking on a deep luster with a hint of a black underpainting . . . I now look out on my neighbor's garage. Here the trees are very young, and seem impermanent. Provisional. I suspect that at night the management company takes them away and puts them in the leasing office. Similarly, the Japanese irises, whose paperiness in my garden suggests delicacy, here suggest merely un-aliveness. The roses have no smell.

Tired of my complaining, a friend of mine says, for God's sake, at least invest in a couple of prints. I tell him I'm too old for that, and I know they'll charge me if I put tape marks on the walls. But then I hunger for an image that is not in any of the books I've brought; I go on Google for a well-made print—not poster size, a more decorous five by eight—of Bernini's *Apollo and Daphne*. The sculpture makes its home in the least domestic of domestic spaces, the Villa Borghese, in my beloved Rome. Because after I leave here, after a brief sojourn in my real home, or homes (about which more later), I will go back to the apartment in Rome, another temporary dwelling that calls up in me feelings as opposite from the ones I am feeling here as it is possible to suggest.

And so I conjure it, my time in Rome, by placing on the wall of the place so different from it, an image of the way I lived there: mornings reading and writing, each afternoon pledged to seeing one beautiful thing, because the place where I lived in Rome was most importantly in Rome. Rome was outside the window beside which I read, but even sitting by the window I was in Rome, and so Rome was part of everything I read and wrote. If it were not a sunny day, the light was insufficient, but I didn't mind it, because, from my chair, inside, protected, private, in the place I had set aside for reading and writing, I had access to the life of the city. A place where people walked the streets not reading and writing but living: buying and selling, cleaning the streets or dirtying them, living their so public lives: in Italian there is no word for privacy.

Unlike my apartment in Palo Alto, the Roman flat was not convenient. One had to walk up four flights of stairs, and they were narrow, and often the light that I pressed at the bottom of the stairs to illuminate the way went off before I got to the top, unless I was really quick. I never seemed to think or wonder about the neighbors, whom I met only once, when the lights went out, and they offered candles and reassured me that this was not a rare occurrence, I must not worry, only I must not expect that the lights would be back on anytime soon.

Here in my California apartment complex, when the garbage disposal stops up, someone comes to fix it in an hour. There was no garbage disposal in Rome, and if it had broken and I had tried to get someone to fix it, I would have been advised, *"Pazienza."* This complex is very quiet; you rarely see anyone out, except in a car. It was outside the Roman windows, especially on weekend nights, and sometimes I even heard the sound of fighting—but I also sometimes, far more often in fact, heard the sound of singing, and when I'd open my doorway at the bottom of the dark stairwell I was treated to a view of peach and ochre and bright yellow walls. I thought of my rooms not as a refuge from the outside world but a part of it. Inside and outside did not fight against each other; they were complements. I could walk to anything I wanted, and although no one knew my name, they always greeted me enthusiastically. Anytime I liked, I could sit beside a great fountain where people have sat for centuries, in front of the basilica, where people have prayed for centuries. The basilica is graced by a Byzantine mosaic beneath which sleep homeless people with their dogs. At the corner is a woman, whom I later discover is French, who sits and does not seem to be begging, her eyes always focused on quite elaborate and quite elegant embroidery, upon which she seems always to be working. Here because human life had made its mark I understood that comfort and happiness are not so simple as some Americans seem to think.

But I am not in Rome, I am in my sterile Palo Alto complex, and I am glad to escape to a speaking engagement in Berkeley, only a few miles away. I will stay in a hotel where I have stayed before, a hotel I love. It is the Berkeley City Club, designed by Julia Morgan, the architect who spent thirty years designing Hearst's Castle in San Simeon. I stayed here a year ago with my daughter, and here, too, I felt immediately at home, completely happy. It does not have all the modern conveniences. There are no televisions in the rooms. The single beds are rather small. There is, in the hallways, particularly as the day progresses, a smell of age and must. Yet my heart soars here. It is an art nouveau production, neo-Gothic; Americans trying to steal the grandeur of a Europe they feel fortunate not to have to live in, not to have to be part of. There are leaded windows with Gothic arches. No wall is entirely square; the line by which it meets the ceiling is a curve. There are tiles embedded in the walls, mostly gray-green, and small medallions of color, almost arbitrary. None of the windows is the same. In the library are books that no one has read for fifty years, but I feel that if I sat there I could write a wonderful book in two weeks. The swimming pool, similar to San Simeon's, lets in light from high windows, some of which are cracked, as is the mirror in my bedroom closet. I could swim and swim forever, my eye resting on the magenta, turquoise, olive-colored tiles, the Moorish shape of the windows. The lock of my room door sticks. Breakfast is not served after nine. Guests are told there is no speaking in the hallways after ten o'clock, except for whispers. The shower's stream is unimpressive. The bathroom is un-large. The light in the closet is worked from a spring that needs to be pulled twice. But there are courtyards where one can sit and hear the sound of water splashing in gentle fountains. A half cloister, leading nowhere, shelters modest primroses and daring, bright geraniums. Birds, looking for refuge in this urban setting, set themselves down skittishly on the pavements where they will not find stray crumbs. Expense was put into materials, the stone, the marble, the tiles, the fountains, but not on what would be called comfort. Yet I am comfortable here, with a deep sense of comfort that once again makes me think I must investigate what the word means for most Americans born in the twentieth century, to say nothing of the twenty-first.

In the middle of my time in California, the time during which I know that I am not at home, I travel to another speaking engagement. I make a journey to participate in a conference in Jerusalem. Jerusalem: Israel, Palestine: the place where the notion of who has the right to inhabit what space is a part of the daily conversation, a conversation that is enacted not only in language but also in bombs and blood. Two peoples who believe the land is theirs, that they have a right to inhabit it, a sacred right, a right that can be traced to a text and to the

bones of forebears who lived and died there. Of this
country the critic Isaiah Berlin has said, "too much
history, too little geography." But the fate of Israel
and Palestine forces us to think about habitation in
a singular way. Why does it matter so much where
you live? What is the importance of the idea of a
homeland? What is the idea the return to which is
so essential that it is worthy of your life, the lives of
your children, and the lives of the children of your
enemy? The Holy Land can only be holy because of
human habitation. And how strange that we should
use the pronoun "my" in front of "land." And to have
the notion that an accident of blood or birth deter-
mines a *right to habitation.* The belief that only on
a particular ground, called a state, *my state,* can one
be safe. A *notion of habitation* that requires for its
identity a defense against an enemy, who believes
he has rights to the same piece of ground.

When I leave this place in California, where I am
not happy, where I am not "at home," and people
ask me where I am going, I will say home, by which
I mean, my New York apartment. But I mean more
than that, because in fact, as a privileged American,
an American at the top 5 percent of privilege,

I long, as does
every human being,
to be at home wherever
I find myself.

—Maya Angelou

I have two homes, both of which, unlike this place I live in now, seem right for me to call home.

My official address, the address to which the IRS sends my taxes, the place where I vote, is on a street on the Upper West Side of Manhattan. The place that has always seemed to me the great good place. When I was growing up, we called it the city, *the city*. During a childhood lived only twenty miles away, I dreamed of it as the place I really belonged. When my father and I would take the train into "the city" and my real life began, I no longer had to pretend to be an impostor: I could now publically be who I privately knew myself to be: A New Yorker, an urban dweller. *Urbane*.

I live in an apartment building . . . sometimes called an apartment house, but it isn't really a house, first of all, because it is too big, and secondly because I share space with my neighbors. We enter the building and walk into something called a foyer, or vestibule. There, the doorman sits, and there the life of the building collects itself. There I watch the children of my neighbors grow from passengers in strollers to willowy adults, as my neighbors watched my children. There I learn that someone's wife has died, and someone else is moving to Chicago. There we have our holiday party, where someone brings a table from upstairs and we share food: those who celebrate Christmas, and those who celebrate Chanukah or Kwanzaa, and those who can only eat after sundown during Ramadan, and those who hate the whole damn thing but like their neighbors. I know that where I live I do not live alone.

My apartment is on the ground floor; I do not have a view; others would be bothered by street noise, but I am not. I have what is most prized to an urban dweller: ample space. Moldings from the nineteenth or early twentieth century, real plaster walls. A bathroom window made of crushed glass. Most important: I open my door to the life of the street, and my place of my work, and then to the park and the river where I can be endlessly refreshed by the glinting light and the changing greens or yellows of the old, venerable trees. And one block to Broadway, where I will be bound to see not only friends but people whose looks I could never have imagined as a child. Sometimes my upstairs neighbor comes and says, "Is your apartment too hot?" and I say, "No, I'm on the ground floor," and we strategize about whom

One never reaches home,
but wherever friendly paths
intersect the whole world
looks like home for a time.

—Herman Hesse

it might make sense to complain to. We are rent-ers; our landlord is the university that is also our employer. Our rents are subsidized; we know we're lucky. We also often don't know who in the enormous University bureaucracy might be of help. We take in each other's mail. When one of my neighbors wins a Nobel Prize, we toast him in the foyer.

But the situation of my New York life under-scores the complexity and inadequacy of the ques-tion: Where do you live? I live in an apartment. But I live in New York, and I sacrifice space to live there, and I pay far more than I would in other places for the same square footage. I live in an apartment in New York in order that I can live the kind of life I want. It makes possible a *style*. I live a life impor-tantly shaped by frequent contact with like-minded friends, a life that gives me access to high culture in a frequent and spontaneous way that is impos-sible if trips to museums, concerts, nonmainstream films must be planned and rationed. I am able to live where I live because my housing is related to my work: it is a benefit of my academic job, and I live steps away from my workplace. In that sense, *my habitation* has more in common with the mix

of private life and public work that has character-
ized the living arrangements of most of my species
throughout most of history.

But I live somewhere else, too. As one of the
ridiculously privileged inhabitants of the planet, I
own what is called a country house. It is the first
house I have ever really loved; perhaps it is more
true to say it is the first house I have ever been in
love with.

As a young woman, I would not have predicted
that I would fall in love with a house. That I would
yearn for it when I am away, as I would a lover.
That I would attend to its needs, anticipating its
afflictions, forestalling them, assuaging them as I
would a child. That it would comfort and solace
me like the perfect mother. Provide the necessary
environment for work: not only my mother but
additionally my patron, my sugar daddy.

For most of my life, I had feared houses:
what they represented, their demands, which I
saw as inimical to my life as an artist. I agreed
with Emerson that gardens were the enemies of
ink wells. My models for domestic life were not
encouraging. There was my grandmother, whose
iron rule over her demesne created a tense *basso*

continuo that poisoned family life. And then my mother who, perhaps in rebellion against her mother, seemed determined to create a shambles. And so for a long time I was afraid of owning any house I might like—a variation of Groucho Marx not wanting to be a member of any club that would have him. I was afraid that I would be inattentive: I would leave the bath running and the walls would turn to chalky milk. I would leave the iron on and the beautiful woodwork would burn to a cinder. I would fail to identify silverfish or earwigs; I would not stop mildew in its tracks.

Perhaps I was never able to love a house because my first house was taken from me, cruelly, violently, and suddenly. My mother and father and I lived on the top floor of a house that was located only three blocks from the house where my mother's mother, my grandmother, had lived since 1920. In that house, my grandmother had raised her nine children, and my mother had lived there from the time she was twelve to the time of her marriage at thirty-nine. We lived on the floor above the family who owned it, a mother and father and three little girls, one of whom I was bullied by, one whom I bullied, one too small for me to take into account.

The parents had been born in Italy; the mother was kind, and often she seemed grieved by the energy expended and demanded by her children; she had deep dark circles under her eyes, and she would wring her hands and urge us to "play nice." The house smelled deliciously of coffee and roasting nuts, of sautéing garlic and rich furniture polish; we played store in the clean, dry basement (unfinished but undangerous) and I, alone in the attic, danced amid the light-saturated dust motes, and dreamed of the family who'd lived before us, whose name was Chamberlain, and who had left behind them a ceramic beer stein with an imprint of a dying stag.

This was the house where I was the child of the family, the child of a mother and a father. This was the house where I had a childhood. And then one night we got a phone call: my father had had a heart attack in the Forty-second Street library. He was taken to Bellevue Hospital; I never saw him again. My uncle came and drove my mother to the hospital; I was taken in my pajamas to sleep in my grandmother's house. A month later my father died, and I never saw our house again. I moved in with my grandmother and my aunt, to a house where it was made quite clear was not ours. Certainly not mine. My punitive, house-proud aunt determined that my toys and dolls "took up too much room," and my precious Alice in Wonderland rug, my wind-up Cinderella and the prince, my baby doll (life-size, with a hard, plastic head) and the baby clothes that I had dressed her in, the china balle-rina with the tutu of starched gauze—were taken somewhere . . . given away or burned, in any case named unprecious and irrelevant.

The house I lived in from seven to eighteen was a house of sadness and conflict. My grandmother died without a will, and the children tore them-selves and one another apart fighting over it. My mother, ostensibly, won the right to live there, but she let the place fall apart, and it became a place of sadness and defeat. I left it happily for various undistinguished student digs that I treated shabbily. Then there was the brief and stressful marriage to the man who made it impossible that I would live at ease in any dwelling where he hung his hat. Because I didn't deserve to live there: in a house.

After my second marriage, I lived for more than a decade in a town along the Hudson River where I did not belong, and I knew that for most of the time I lived there. I had moved into the house there when I married the man who is now my husband, the father of my children. It was there my babies were conceived and nursed and reared; loved friends were fed and hosted there . . . and yet I never felt that it was mine. I cannot tell you why. It was a well-built house, light-filled and of admirable character. My husband had rescued that house from a wreck, and it was dear to him. I don't quite understand why that house never felt like mine; perhaps it was that the landscape—mountains that always seemed to me overly male and forbidding—did not seem to welcome me. I thought perhaps the problem was with houses and me. It took me much longer than it should have to say: I want another house, a house where I belong. It was only after I was able to say this sentence that I found the house with which I fell in love.

It is, as I have suggested, unlikely that I would ever fall in love with a house. But if the situation is unlikely, the story of my finding it is more unlikely still; it has about it aspects of the miraculous.

When I told my husband I wanted to sell the house in the Mid–Hudson Valley because I wanted a house in a place I loved, I had hoped for a house near the ocean, in the Cape Cod town where we had summered for a quarter of a century. This was a hope, or a dream, that was not to be realized. A house we had rented for many years, a house I loved, came on the market. It had belonged to a brave and talented woman, a writer who had lived simply and imaginatively. She had done beautiful things with the house, not by great capital investment, but because her eye was flexible and lively. She came to Cape Cod at a time when one could buy property, even houses, cheaply. It was a haven for artists and writers. But by the time her children wanted to sell the house, by the time it was offered to me, Cape Cod was a place that artists and writers (except for the millionaires among them) could no longer afford. Doctors and lawyers, hedge fund managers, were buying and building there; looking for something I could afford, I learned of an unexceptional two-bedroom house, built in the sixties and abutting a dog kennel, that went for three quarters of a million dollars. I understood that I could only buy the beautiful house that had once belonged to the brave imaginative writer by distorting my own life with financial anxieties and pressures that would make a mockery of everything I said that I believed was important. To buy the house that I had summered in, a house that was a dream of ease and freedom, I would have to become its slave, twisting my life as a writer to feed its hungry maw.

In my grief, I fixated on what I couldn't have, and didn't hear what three different friends were telling me: look elsewhere, in this place where we have settled, something of a secret . . . and affordable. The name of the place had no resonance for me, however, so I could not listen.

Then one day, soon after September 11, I was walking my dog in the park near my home. The dog owners who use the park have negotiated with the police: we can walk our dogs off lead between six and nine in the mornings and after nine at night. My dog made the acquaintance of another dog. They engaged in a fine and all-absorbing romp. The other dog's owner remarked on the felicity of dogs being allowed to run off lead in the park. "You're not from here," I said. He said he was from the place people had been telling me to look for the house of my dreams. I mentioned the oddness of it to him, and he named a real estate website. This is a joke, as I am a famous computer-phobe, but feeling I'd been addressed by an angel, I ran home and looked on the website. I was amazed! There were attractive properties that I knew I could afford . . . desirable houses that were of the same value as the house I did not love that I was determined now to sell.

I phoned the real estate agent. The house I'd been interested in had been sold, but she said she'd fax me descriptions of other properties. I drove there one Saturday on a lark. When I approached the house, I was disappointed. It was painted a dull mustard color, grim and uninviting. But then approaching it more closely, and walking around its single acre, I became enchanted by the old grand trees, the stone walls, the boulders jutting up out of the grass, making their point that a suburban lawn was entirely out of the question. The Realtor opened the door and I walked in. The light fell on my shoulders, warmed the top of my head. I sat down at the dining room table; I had to sit, I had been struck a devastating blow. "This is my house," I said. "I have to have it."

The Realtor mentioned an obstacle. Someone else was interested. They had first dibs. If they were no longer interested, we could speak.

I went home, desolated. Two days later, the Realtor called. As it turned out, those others were unable to raise the necessary cash. Could I arrange for a mortgage immediately . . . to preempt their attempts to come up with the necessary down payment. I phoned some banks; in twenty minutes, I was a mortgagee.

So why, the minute that I entered this house, did I feel I could put my fears and misgivings behind me, relax in the embrace of this lover, mother, patron, child? Was it the high windows, insisting on their extravagance of light? It had been originally a schoolhouse; built in 1870, the windows were there for the illumination of childish minds; their old glass seemed to give new meaning to the word "transparency." Nothing would be hidden here; no dark secrets, no lurking nightmares. And the house: so solid that the appraiser almost fell to his knees in admiration. Here is another aspect of the miraculous to which the house attaches. It had been the project of a young couple who had devoted ten years to rescuing it from the desecration of half a century. The Realtor showed me pictures of cramped dark rooms, linoleum-covered floors, wallpaper that looked like the effluvia of some dank rodent. This couple had taken down walls and put down wooden floors; they had redone the old windows, finding replacement panes that kept the feeling of the old but insulating the windows so they kept out drafts and whistling wind; they had strengthened the foundations and installed a new furnace. They had started a garden. And then, having done all this, they had split up—the husband moving to California, the wife to the state of Washington. They had, it seemed, done it all for me.

And they had left in charge of the garden a neighbor whose easy love of what grew enabled me to ask, without anxiety and shame, the simple questions that are necessary if one is going to begin from ignorance. Now, I take pleasure in my garden. What was there before me . . . three varieties of lilac: white, the customary lavender, an older purple the color of grape jam. A vegetable garden where I grow tomatoes, basil, lettuce, arugula, . . . and plant accompanying marigolds to keep away bad bugs. The room where I write has a window that overlooks a tree, a tree with the unglamorous name of pignut hickory, venerable, spreading like Longfellow's chestnut, with a dappled shadowy bark and leaves whose progress I follow with a lifting of

Peace—that was the other name for home.

—Kathleen Norris

the heart in spring, a thudding dread at the approach of winter. It is my tree; its fate is my fate. . . .

In this house I am happy . . . it is mine, nothing in it is there to vex me or give me pain. It wants to cause me the minimum of trouble. The light in the morning welcomes me and soothes me into the demands of the day; on the porch I watch the sun set and the geese fly in their determined V: I learn a secret from them, that geese take turns being leaders, when one is tired he goes to the back of the formation, a new, rested, member taking up his place. The area around my house is the one place on earth where I never get lost. On my birthday, the gardener, now a treasured friend, toasted me and said, "It's as if the house was always waiting for you to come home."

A complex in California. An art nouveau hotel. A Roman house overlooking bell towers and a piazza. The city of Jerusalem. A ground-floor New York flat. A reconverted schoolhouse in New England. I begin thinking about what it is to live someplace, how it is that we live where we live . . . and why it matters.

two

Money,
Morals, History,
Symbol, Safety

As I am thinking in this way, I am bombarded with the news of a crashing economy. An economy that I have to understand is crashing because of something called "subprime mortgages." A phrase that for a very long time has no meaning for me. What I can understand: the economy has crashed, airbrushing greed and random malice, largely because of a fantasy of how we, as Americans, must live.

It is, oddly enough, an idea that united both right and left: Barney Frank, the ultraliberal Massachusetts congressman, agreed with President George Bush on this issue; supporters of business deregulation joined hands with radical inner-city activists in the belief that everyone should own his or her own home. Everyone should own his or her own home because, the idea goes, homeownership has a moral valence.

In a recent *New York Times* column, Nobel Prize–winning economist Paul Krugman noted this connection. "Listening to politicians, you'd think that every family should own its home—in fact, that you're not a real American unless you're a homeowner. 'If you own something,' Mr. Bush once declared, 'you have a vital stake in the future of our country.' Presumably, then, citizens who live in rented housing, and therefore lack that 'vital stake,' can't be properly patriotic. Bring back property qualifications for voting!"[2]

The connection of homeownership and morality is not new. The eighteenth-century philosopher Immanuel Kant said: "The house, the residence, is the only rampart against the dread of barbarian darkness, and the obscurity of the past. Its walls contain all that mankind has patiently amassed over hundreds of centuries. It opposes escape, loss and absence by erecting an internal order, a civility, a passion of its own. Its liberty flourishes where there is stability and finitude, not openness and infinity. To be at home is to recognize life's slow pace and the pleasures of sedentary meditation. . . . Man's identity is thus residential and that is why the revolutionary, who has neither hearth nor home, hence neither faith nor law, epitomizes the anguish of errancy. . . . The man without a home is a potential criminal."[3]

How strange this passionate advocacy of home-ownership on the part of Kant, someone who lived alone, never had guests, and insisted upon only owning one piece of art so that he wouldn't be distracted. This hyper-rationalist was a victim of the romance of the house, the notion that moral and intellectual life is best nurtured by a structure that makes an important distinction between private and public life.

Taking a particularly Italian slant on the implications of habitation, the literary critic and inveterate collector of beautiful objects, Mario Praz (1896–1982) said, with the robustness of diction not

A house is not a home unless
it contains food and fire for
the mind as well as the body.

—Benjamin Franklin

unfamiliar to his compatriots, "'He doesn't care about houses,' is in my lexicon a statement as serious and final as, in the lexicon of a moralist, an essential lack of ethical sense would be. . . . The man who has no sense of the house and who is not moved by the harmony of handsome furnishings is for me, as for Shakespeare, the man who 'hath no music in himself, a man fat for treasons, stratagems and spoils. The motions of his spirit are dull as night, and his affections dark as Erebus.' Let no such man be trusted!"[4]

And yet, for most of the history of the species, people have not lived in houses that would be remotely recognizable to our notions of what constitutes a house: that is to say, a dwelling that is readily understood as separate from the dwellings of others and separated from the outside world. A place in that privacy is enabled, in which cleanliness is accomplished, in which safety is assured. The kind of house that Barney Frank and George Bush—as well as Martha Stewart—had in mind is really a product of seventeenth-century Holland.

Such a powerful idea emanating from such a small country such a long time ago. How, I wondered, did all this come to be? What were we looking for in a place to live? What could it provide? What was it that we required?

It would seem that the first and most obvious thing we ask from the places we live is that they keep us safe.

We are, as a species, terrifyingly fragile, ill-equipped for what nature provides in the way of dangers: cold, heat, storm, predatory beasts—arguably the most dangerous of which are those of our own kind. Perhaps the house, the idea of a house, the geometries of a house, its architectural details are a poignant sign of our touching belief that we can be safe in a universe that does not privilege our safety above that of other species or seem to notice that we are vulnerable to natural forces that range from the tsunami to the termite.

As an instance of delusional thinking, let's take the example of the lock. The lock, as Gaston Bachelard points out, is much more metaphor than actual protection. "The lock doesn't exist that could resist absolute violence, and all locks are an invitation to thieves. A lock is a psychological threshold."[5] A sign more than a shield.

Yet we believe in them, as we believe in so much that makes it possible to live. It occurs to me that those eminently practical types—architects, engineers, bankers—are involved in one of the most pervasive fantasies common to human kind: the idea that there is somewhere we can be safe. And yet, without this fiction how could we go on?

This powerful fiction has generated its own culture: its own language, its own economy, its own manners, its own laws. On the subject of language, consider, for example, the touchingly hopeful concept: Homeland Security. Homeland; what is conjured up by this word? Ma and Pa, she in a flowered apron, he in overalls, his toil-worn hands caked with the traces of the good earth he tills. But what was permitted under the rubric "homeland security" was an increased and increasingly technological surveillance that was probably of little use in protecting us from enemies whose weapons could be hidden in a pocket or a shoe.

Modern middle-class people living in the Western hemisphere, at least its northern half, are probably safer from what might be constituted as dangerous than most other groups of people living in most of the history of the world. And yet we feel unsafe, and our houses reflect this feeling. I am always struck by the number of terms, representing a number of new realities that we grow to think of as commonplace. Who, thirty years ago, had heard of the phrase "gated community"? And who, when I was growing up, knew anyone whose house was equipped with a burglar alarm? Statistics reported by the *Washington Post* in 2005 report that in 1970, a negligible number of homes were equipped with burglar alarms; by 1979 they were in 2 percent of homes. In 1992 the figure was 20 percent, and in 2005 the percentage had risen to 32 percent.

Surprisingly, the increase in the number of home security systems was not a result of an increase in the number of burglaries. According to the annual National Crime Victimization Survey conducted by the Bureau of Justice Statistics, 29.8 of every 1,000 households were burglarized in 2003, compared with 58.2 per 1,000 households in 1993, 84 per 1,000 in 1983, and 110 per 1,000 in 1973.[6]

It would certainly be possible to speculate that the lower rate of burglaries is a result of the greater preponderance of alarms. But is there a deeper reason for their popularity? The notion that, not only can technology keep us safe, but that we are unsafe without it. I am the owner of a home alarm.

I would be uneasy if someone suggested that I give it up. Do I need it now more than I needed it in 1970? Or less? It doesn't matter. I think I need it. I think I need it to keep me safe.

Talleyrand noted that "the citizen's life must be walled off."[7] But walled off from what? Once again, our notions of safety, like our notions of danger, are culturally determined. Our earliest forebears had to think hard about protecting themselves from really threatening animals, not Fido or Whiskers, whom we invite onto our couches and provide with their own embroidered pillows. Then there were those folks who had to invest a certain sizable amount of capital on things like moats. For these privileged men, their home was not only their castle, their castle was their fortress. Many of us find it increasingly difficult to give up the fortress model, and the home-security industry is the beneficiary of this habit of mind.

It could be argued that the move from urban to suburban areas has a double motivation. People want more space. And they want to feel safe.

But safe from whom? Those others considered dangerous. Sometimes they are named: the poor, the darker skinned. Those prone to violent crime.

These fears were not entirely unfounded, or simply based on racist paranoia, although they certainly added to the thickness of the racist broth. A lawn, a picket fence: they were the living metaphor for the idea that the world was the family. The nuclear family. Mom and Dad and two or three kids. The only ones with whom it was possible to feel really safe.

The idea that the outside world was dangerous in both physical and moral terms was not an invention of the Wonder bread fifties. As the Renaissance progressed in Western Europe, a tendency to separate work and domestic life became increasingly more robust, its grip firmly in place by the beginning of the seventeenth century. As work moved increasingly into the public sphere, and men had to go outside to make the money to create the home, the outside world, that is, the world outside the home, began increasingly to be seen as the place of moral danger. For men, the danger came from the coarsening habits of commerce, the elbows-out stance that growing capitalism required, the toleration, or encouragement, of dishonesty that home was a haven from. Speaking of the home-loving Dutch of the

seventeenth century, historian Simon Schama
remarks that the family household

> *was the crucible through which rude*
> *matter and beastly appetite could*
> *be transubstantiated into redeeming*
> *wholesomeness. When food, lust, sloth,*
> *indolence and vain luxury were subdued*
> *by the domestic virtues—sobriety, frugality,*
> *piety, humility, aptitude and loyalty—they*
> *were deprived of their dirt, which is to*
> *say, their capacity for inflicting harm or*
> *jeopardizing the soul. Home was that morally*
> *purified and carefully patrolled terrain where*
> *license was governed by prudence, and the*
> *wayward habits of animals, children and*
> *footloose unmarried women were subdued*
> *into a state of harmony and grace.*[8]

If home was the place where men had to be protected from themselves, or where their baser
natures had to go for disinfection, it was, for
women, the only safeguard for the treasure of their
virtue. In return for being kept from the outside
world, women were given the rule of the inside. By

the seventeenth century, this division of the imagination—outside = male, and dangerous; inside = female, and safe—had hardened and solidified. The rationale: the world was a dangerous place. Only home was safe.

This understanding, however, fails to take account of the situation of those disproportionately women, for whom the home is the least safe place on earth. Most sexual abuse occurs at home; domestic violence is the largest killer of women in the very world that calls itself civilized.

And if houses don't keep us safe from other humans, do they keep us safe from the ravages of nature?

Human beings have not always been entirely rational in choosing the sites most naturally conducive to their safety. Take, for example, Northern California. Living there as I have just been doing, but perhaps more crucially having had a daughter who lived there, I could not fail to pay attention to something called a fault line. Suddenly, there came into my consciousness a new gerund: earthquake-proofing.

I had to believe that it was possible: that buildings, houses could be earthquake-proof. I had to believe it because people I loved were living on the fault line.

I did not believe it for a minute.

Did the people of New Orleans believe that the water would not raise its banks? That the levees would hold? That it would not happen again? Having seen everything they love float away, could they ever again believe in the possibility of a safe haven?

And what if nature is not safe from us?

Considering the question of habitation, it is important that we think of ourselves not only as victims, but also potential victimizers. Our desire to inhabit, to distance ourselves from our fellows, to place our homes in a beautiful landscape, has destroyed hundreds and thousands of acres of wilderness, and the effect of this might result in the destruction of the place that we all believe ourselves right to call home: planet earth. Our yearning for larger, more comfortable homes has led to an increase in the demand for resources that jeopardize every possible aspect of our lives, resulting in the threat of an uninhabitable world.

And even our houses are not safe from us. There is, of course, simple neglect. It is not difficult to call up the example of a fine house whose lines have been ruined by carelessness or a failure of aesthetic attentiveness. Cedar shingles replaced by aluminum siding. Classical entrances betrayed by a circular drive. Cherry wood floors covered by linoleum or carpeting the color of dead mice. Majestic oaks cut down to make room for a hot tub.

And then there is the damage caused by the failure to understand the care a house requires.

I once visited a great house in Newport, Rhode Island, whose greatness was destroyed by the whim of a reckless pair of women: a mother and a daughter; the daughter, a successful nightclub singer. In 1941, they bought a great house, Rosecliff, designed by Stanford White on the model of the Grand Trianon of Versailles. The owners of the house had to give it up, having lost their fortune in the Depression. The mother bought it for her daughter's twenty-first birthday. Mother and daughter lived in the house for one summer. Then they left it, forgetting to drain the pipes, which burst in the winter, destroying the house, encasing the heart-shaped staircase in ice. They left Rosecliff a ruin and then sold it at a profit . . . having bought it, it was said heartlessly, for "a song."

I live in my house as I live inside my skin: I know more beautiful, more ample, more sturdy and more picturesque skins: but it would seem to me unnatural to exchange them for mine.

—Primo Levi

And sometimes houses are victims of a malice we intend not toward them but toward other human beings. Take, for instance, the history of a house in a small town in Spain I once visited. It was a white stucco farmhouse with an orange tiled roof, perhaps a hundred years old, simple, but beautifully placed in a grove of almond trees. From the site of the house, there was a magnificent view of the Mediterranean and its surrounding hills; the sounds of birds wheeling and cawing filled your ears. In it lived an extended family: two brothers and their wives, and their assorted children. Some friction developed between the wives; a breach occurred. The only solution the brothers could think of was to build a crude partition of concrete blocks separating the two families, ensuring that they wouldn't even have to see each other. Eventually, on the death of one of the brothers, one side of the house became available and it was bought by an American and his Dutch wife. (The pair did a brilliant job of restoring their half of the house, planting and repairing, painting, installing a new well. The other half was taken over by one of the sons of the family who was a drug addict. His half of the house turned into a monstrosity;

he regularly fell asleep and the walls were scarred by fires; his unclean dishes attracted vermin. One half a triumph of imagination, one half a disaster. What Keats would call an objective correlative of what can be done for or to a house.

We own our houses but we owe them. We cannot for long look away without some tragedy we may not even have known how to name.

For all these reasons, it seems to me an act of simultaneous courage and folly to attach one's heart to anyplace we live. Our trust in it as the good mother: huge, impermeable, implacable: how childish, how touchingly absurd. How can we close a door, which, after all, is only a breach in a wall, and think that we are safe? From the violence of our enemies. The impersonal rages and caprices of a nature that cares nothing for our little lives or may be taking its revenge for our betrayals. From our fear of the outside, and the outsider. From our families. Ourselves.

Perhaps the one thing houses really keep us safe from is the eyes of others. And so privacy and safety are linked. Houses allow us the safety of doing those things we would rather not be seen doing, or even wanting to do.

Of the structural elements that make up the house, perhaps the most important is the door, which can be opened, yes, but perhaps more crucially closed. The door is the machine, or mark, that separates us from the world. Simon Schama speaks of the door frame as marking the distinction between home and the world, between safety within and unknown without.[9] Mario Praz notes, "The house is the sphere of influence, the vital space, the fief, the domain, the allodium, or whatever other expression that lawgivers and politicians may be pleased to coin, to signify what, in the child's primary language is expressed with a petulant 'that's mine.'"[10]

But any parent understands that the words "that's mine," enclose within them their corollary: "it's not yours."

A house encloses, but also closes out. Without the invention of the door, there would have been no possibility for intimacy. When we think of intimacy, it is not an ideal of inclusion that comes to mind; for intimacy to happen, some must be allowed in, others kept out. Intimacy. Privacy. How easily the words come to us, how automatic, as categories, they seem. But what do we mean by privacy? It is one of our most cherished, most contested rights: "The right to privacy." But what exactly do we mean by privacy? Or private life?

What we think of as the private life is of necessity quite culturally specific. Our notions of private space differ from a Japanese, or a Masai, or a Navajo. I once met a Chinese writer who was appalled that, in coming to New York, he was given his own apartment. How, he wondered, could people be so heartless as to leave him entirely on his own? What would happen to him if he became sick or injured? He understood the oppressive qualities of the constant surveillance of Chinese life, but at least, he said, he never felt alone. After a year of living on his own in America though, he found it painfully jarring to return to a more communal style of life.

In addition to being geographically specific, our notions of privacy have a rather recent historical vintage. In his magisterial study, *A History of Private Life,* Philippe Ariès notes that our notion of privacy is linked with the notion of the individual. He dates the growth of the idea of both to the period between 1500 and 1800. In those years, he states, "people began to imagine, experience, and protect private life in a new way."

In his much more modest and far more accessible book *Home*, architect Witold Rybczynski makes the same point. He notes that words such as "self confidence," "self esteem," "melancholy," and "sentimental" appeared in English and French only two or three hundred years ago.[11] Their use marked the emergence of something new in human consciousness: the appearance of the internal world of the individual, of the self and of the family.

It would seem that this idea, or ideal, of privacy and intimacy is dependent on the idea and the reality of rooms. Ariès says that for this ideal to become a reality, what is required is "a space outside society that can provide solitude, secrecy, and silence. The garden, the bedroom (with its alcoves and recesses), the study, and the library filled the need, hiding what could not and should not be seen (care of the body, natural functions, the act of love) and offering a place for practices more than ever associated with isolation, such as prayer and reading."[12]

But such spaces were a long time coming. For most of the history of the West (ancient Greece and Rome being exceptions), masters and servants, parents and children lived in a room without divisions; work, the preparation and consumption of food, bathing, and sleeping took place in one open space. Until the sixteenth century, even the wealthy lived life publicly; the hallway, for example, was unknown even in royal palaces such as Hampton Court: remodeled by William and Mary in the late seventeenth century. Servants passing from room to room had to go through each room in turn. In discussing a woodcut of St. Jerome by the sixteenth-century artist Albrecht Durer, Witold Rybczynski notes the anomaly of the depiction of the scholar-saint's study, noting that in that period it was unusual, even for a scholar-saint, to have his own room.[13] The reality of centuries of habitation without designated rooms causes the mind to spin. What kind of people have sex in the same room, perhaps the same bed, as their children? What kind of people go to the bathroom in the presence of others? What kind of people bathe in the same place where they eat, exchange money, sign contracts? Whatever we say, we know they were different from us, and the differences raise questions that make us reel: how did they live, who were they? Whoever they were, they were people without our deeply rooted understanding of the rightness, the propriety of certain kinds of enclosures for certain kinds of activities.

The anthropologist Mary Douglas marvels at the tenacity of such perceptions in her book *Purity and Danger: An Analysis of Concepts of Pollution and Taboo.* She says:

> *I am personally rather tolerant of disorder. But I always remember how unrelaxed I felt in a particular bathroom which was kept spotlessly clean in so far as the removal of grime and grease was concerned. It had been installed in an old house in a space created by the simple expedient of setting a door at each end of a corridor between two staircases. The décor remained unchanged: the engraved portrait of Vinogradoff, the books, the gardening tools, the row of gumboots. It all made good sense as the scene of a back corridor, but as a bathroom— the impression destroyed repose. . . . In chasing dirt, in papering, decorating, tidying we are not governed by anxiety to escape disease, but are positively re-ordering our*

environment, making it conform to
an idea.[14]

Intrigued by this idea, the distinguished anthro-pologist ill at ease in a makeshift bathroom, I immediately Google Vinogradoff and discover that he was a Russian thinker who specialized in an understanding of peasant life. Peasants, for whom the concept of room, to say nothing of bathroom, would be incomprehensible.

And so for Douglas, an essential universal human impulse is the desire to order and to shape our environment. But such ordering and reordering is importantly connected to an idea of separation and distinction. The idea of privacy, like the idea of the individual, is importantly founded on the habit of separation. Think of the names of rooms that we consider commonplace: kitchen, bathroom, bed-room, living room, dining room. But then there are others, which might easily be considered luxury items: study, library, music room, den. Why do we think we have to be in a separate or different place to do particular or different things? Do we think that calling something different will make the task easier? More important?

There is a magic in that little world, home; it is a mystic circle that surrounds comforts and virtues never known beyond its hallowed limits.

—Robert Southey

It is, no doubt, an illusion, but it is a powerful one, in whose grip I understand myself to be, as I close my study door with a decisive, if not aggressive, click. I have never understood the appeal of loft living. I think of a line in one of my favorite movies, *A Thousand Clowns*. The hero, Murray Burns, says to his nephew, Nick, "Go to your room." "But, Murray," he says, "it's a one-room apartment." "Then go to your alcove," says Murray. The child does: an alcove being enough of a sign of separation or specialness.

Specialness, but also possession. Possession, and also separation. Mario Praz has reminded us that one of the important functions of a house is to enable us to use the word "mine." But it is also important that we be able to use the words "here, not there."

The concept of privacy implies the concept of an individual who wishes to be part of the time invisible. But why? Why do we wish not to be seen? Perhaps more precisely, what is it that we wish not to be seen doing?

The right to privacy is a right to secrecy. Or secrets. But a need for secrecy suggests, necessarily, shame and fear. The fear of judgment and the attendant shame resulting from it.

Should we wish for an ideal world in which there were no need for secrecy, and therefore no need for privacy? This point is made by all totalitarian regimes and for that reason alone it horrifies. The contemporary theologian John Hick imagines that in heaven there will be no barriers between people, therefore no secrets. This is, I must admit, far from my idea of paradise.

But why are secrets so precious? What is so valuable, or fragile, that it needs to be kept from sight? Is it that, like a mother carrying the fledgling young inside her womb, we carry in us ideas that, brought to birth, to light too soon would wither or grow into monstrosities? Our dreams need the couvade of noninterruption.

How strong it is, our wish not to be interrupted. How deeply connected for many of us are the ideas of peace and privacy. Peace is noninterruption. Peace is the community's understanding that one's focus should be inviolate, the creation of an imaginary bubble that makes impermeable the barrier between the self and the world.

Gaston Bachelard insists that one of the most important functions of a house, of the rooms of a house is that, not only is it the place where we do things, it is also the place where we do nothing. The place of rest. The place of secrets and of dreams. "If I were asked to name the chief benefit of the house," he says, "I should say: the house shelters day-dreaming,"[15] the house protects the dreamer, the house allows one to dream in peace.

What kind of privacy is most important to us? The answer to that question—if it could be answered honestly—would be a good index of who we really are, if we understand that who we are can be measured by what is important to us, what we pay for, what we think we cannot live without.

And so, let's ask the question: What is the one place in the contemporary house where one can count on privacy? On not being interrupted? The answer is of course the bathroom. It is not only for hygiene that we retire there. "A bathroom," W. H. Auden reminds us, in his poem "Thanksgiving for a Habitat," "has only an inside lock."[16] One wants to lock oneself in the bathroom, but how horrifying to be locked in by someone else. One's host. One's enemy. One's parent. One's lover. Forced to exist as a citizen in the country devoted to pretending we are not dirty animals; that we do not stink.

If I were asked to name the chief benefit of the house, I should say: the house shelters day-dreaming, the house protects the dreamer, the house allows one to dream in peace.

—Gaston Bachelard

In her book *The Dirt on Clean: An Unsanitized History,* Katherine Ashenburg tells us about an advertisement she saw in the *New York Times Magazine* for an apartment in the Stanhope Hotel, across from the Metropolitan Museum in New York. It was an eight-bedroom apartment; it included eleven bathrooms. Including two for the master bedroom. "At the Stanhope," she says, "Harriet Beecher Stowe's futuristic dream of a bathroom for every two or three inhabitants has nearly been turned on its head: this apartment could well accommodate an inhabitant for every two or three bathrooms. . . . 24 per cent of the U.S. houses built in 2005 had three or more bathrooms."[17]

Not two or more libraries, two or more studies, two or more music rooms. Show us your bathroom and we'll tell you who you are.

In the same poem in which he made the point about bathrooms and locks, W. H. Auden, who was famously filthy and known for living in unimaginable chaos, approaches the subject of cleanliness from several angles, all interesting. It is odd, he notes, that "the English, a rather dirty people/ should have invented the slogan,/*Cleanliness is next to Godliness.*"[18] He describes the kind of room in which he feels comfortable, and provides telling details on the kinds of situation in which he is not comfortable at all.

> *spotless rooms*
> *where nothing's left lying about*
> *chill me, so do cups used for ash-trays or smeared*
> *with lip-stick: the homes I warm to,*
> *though seldom wealthy, always convey a feeling*
> *of bills being promptly settled*
> *with cheques that don't bounce.*[19]

He also speaks to the issue of the cultural relativism of cleanliness, perceiving how puzzled Romans would be by our bathrooms, "mistake them for hideouts/warrens of some outlawed sect/who mortify their flesh with strange/implements."[20] In the classical world, bathing was public and people oiled, rather than soaped themselves. Christianity was bad for cleanliness; the widespread practice of public bathing was feared by the Christians to lead to licentiousness, and our medieval forebears were a lot dirtier than their ancient counterparts.

Mary Douglas notes that dirt is essentially disorder: "There is no such thing as absolute dirt; it exists in the eye of the beholder. Nor can our ideas about disease account for our behavior in cleaning or avoiding dirt. Dirt offends against disorder. Eliminating it is not a negative movement, but a positive effort to organize the environment. But to organize it how: to organize it not only into categories of like and unlike but into dangerous and undangerous."[21]

If we agree with Douglas that there is no such thing as absolute dirt, we must agree that there is no such thing as absolute cleanliness, and that different cultures focus on different aspects of it. The seventeenth-century Dutch, for example, were perceived by all other countrymen as being almost phobically careful about the spotlessness of their houses, including attending to the shininess of their stoops. But they were noted by the same observers to pay little attention to the cleanliness of their bodies. You could eat off their floors, but you didn't want to stand too close to the householders. Americans are notoriously critical of Europeans' failure to use deodorant; Europeans are shocked by the absence in our bathrooms of bidets. We associate cleanliness with an absence of visible grime and invisible germs; much of the history of architecture is concerned with separating cooking smells from the parts of the house that were considered living quarters.

And so, as good cultural relativists, we say that we understand that there is no such thing as absolute cleanliness. We nod soberly, aware of the malign effects of ignoring and failing to respect "difference." But when it comes to cleanliness, we can't walk it like we talk it, and certainly we don't put our money where we would fear to put our noses, or more importantly, our mouths. Even when we don't want to, our body responds as if there were a platonic form of cleanliness, the deviation from which is a danger and a threat. In that, as Douglas points out, we are no different from our brothers and sisters in other spots on the globe whom we feel comfortable referring to as "primitive."

In 1956, a University of Michigan professor named Horace Miner published a paper in the *American Anthropologist* called "Body Ritual among the Nacirema." A little-studied group, the Nacirema had a sophisticated market economy, but were most notable for their extraordinary focus on their health and appearance. Their fundamental belief, Miner wrote, was "that the human body is ugly and that its natural tendency is to debility and disease." Imprisoned in these treacherous bodies, the Nacirema resorted to elaborate rituals and extreme behaviors that took place in a household shrine of shrines.

"The more powerful individuals in the society have several shrines in their houses," Miner reported, "and, in fact, the opulence of a house is often referred to in terms of the number of such ritual centers it possesses." The center of the shrine was a chest built into the wall, full of charms and potions. Underneath this charm box was a small font into which flowed holy waters whose purity was guarded by a priestly class. The Nacirema entered the shrine daily, one by one, bowing the head before the charm box and performing a brief ablution ritual. These practices, although critically important to them, were enacted not as a family, but privately and surreptitiously. "The rites are normally only discussed with children," Miner wrote, "and then only during the period when they are being initiated into these mysteries."[22]

The Nacirema are, of course, ourselves: Americans . . . as much in the grips as any other human collectivity of our irrational beliefs. Of course, we can't pretend that Louis Pasteur never lived, and that we never learned anything about microbes. And yet it is possible that our phobia about germs has actually rendered us less healthy. Some research shows that children who are exposed to a certain percentage of germs are healthier than those who are vigilantly protected from it with our insistence on antibacterial soap and a myriad of other products.

The knowledge of germ theory, the increase in the availability of a plentiful supply of water in the private home, the separation of the home and the workplace as different spheres—the latter presided over by women—came together in the nineteenth century. If the woman's place was in the home, its cleanliness was seen as her responsibility; its lack of cleanliness as shame whose lineaments were perceived as a kind of sexual indecency.

There is an inexorable connection between capitalism's need to create new desires that will be the fuel for the creation of new products, and our beliefs about what it is we really need. My grandmother's cleaning products were limited to soap, ammonia, vinegar, and perhaps Bon Ami cleanser, whose label I liked because of the chicken coming

Home is a place not only of strong affections, but of entire unreserved; it is life's undress rehearsal, its backroom, its dressing room, from which we go forth to more careful and guarded intercourse, leaving behind us much debris of cast-off and everyday clothing.

—Harriet Beecher Stowe

out of a well-drawn egg. I remember the introduc-
tion into our family life of Spic and Span, which my
mother thought a fine thing and my grandmother a
frivolity. Later on my aunt, with whom I lived and
whose punitive cleaning has turned me against the
activity for good, discovered Mr. Clean. But now, I
feel compelled to have, under my sink, Fantastik,
Soft Scrub, a special cleaner for the bathtub and
shower, and one for the toilet, though I refuse to
dye the water blue. This proliferation of products is
at least partly based on bringing to women's attention different areas of filth that require different
techniques—and, of course, different products
that can provide a heretofore unknown standard
of purity. And so women are in a constant state
of anxiety, a constant fear of inadequacy, about all
the little nooks and crannies where disease might
be being bred . . . and it is up to them to keep the
demons back. It is a cliché that labor-saving devices
in fact create more labor, but to this I would add
that the number of cleaning products that suggest
they make it easier to keep our houses clean and
healthy in fact invent new time-consuming tasks.
The consumers of the product are women. What is
consumed, disproportionately, is women's time.

What is the relationship between cleanliness and comfort? We all know, or at least have heard of, hostesses who ruin a meal by whisking the dirty dishes away before the meal—or at least the conversation—is ended. Many middle-class houses include rooms where the family is not allowed—except on special occasions when someone outside the family is present. The problem is: human beings are machines for producing, among other things, filth and disorder. If cleanliness is next to godliness, is it next to happiness? Or comfort?

And what, exactly, is comfort? Like privacy and cleanliness, it is a concept that is not only culturally, but historically determined. Witold Rybczynski tells us:

> *"Comfortable" did not originally refer to*
> *enjoyment or contentment. Its Latin root was*
> confortare—*to strengthen or console—and*
> *this remained its meaning for centuries. . . .*
> *This idea of support was eventually*
> *broadened to include people and things*
> *that afforded a measure of satisfaction,*
> *and "comfortable" came to mean tolerable*
> *or sufficient. . . . Succeeding generations*

> *expanded this idea of convenience, and*
> *eventually "comfortable" acquired its sense*
> *of physical well-being and enjoyment, but*
> *not until the eighteenth century. . . . Later*
> *meanings of the word were almost exclusively*
> *concerned with contentment, often of a*
> *thermal variety: "comforter" in secular*
> *Victorian England no longer referred to the*
> *Redeemer, but to a long woolen scarf; today it*
> *describes a quilted bed coverlet.*[23]

"A Clean, Well-Lighted Place." The title of a story by Ernest Hemingway would seem to suggest the minimum of what could even generously be called comfort. And taking a cue from Rybczynski, we might expand the minimum definition to read "a clean, warm, well-lighted place." We have seen that what we middle-class Americans think of as "cleanliness" is a relatively recent acquisition or accomplishment, and this is true as well for warmth and light. Rybczynski divides the history of domestic technology into two major phases: all the years leading up to 1890, and then what followed. He perceives that "all the modern devices that contribute to our domestic comfort—central heating, indoor plumbing, running hot and cold water, electric light and power—were unavailable before 1890 and were well-known by 1920."[24]

But whatever the source or history of the idea of comfort, it would seem to be connected with some real or fantasized or idealized notion of the body's natural state, a way of being that eschews constraint and the unspontaneous. Comfort is the antidote for the discontents imposed upon us by civilization. And this is why we need a dwelling with walls and doors to achieve comfort: society demands that in public we are regularly uncomfortable. That we live our public lives in a consistent acceptance of discomfort. Think of the clothes that we wear: neckties for men, high heels and hose for women. Shirts, skirts, pants, jackets that constrict our waists and rib cages. One of the first things most people do when entering the house is to take their shoes off . . . or at least to exchange the footwear of the street for the footwear of the home. "Sit up straight" is one of the first commands children learn; slouching is a clear gestural indication of moral laxity and fiscal untrustworthiness. But think of the phrase "easy chair." What is an easy chair but a machine that allows the spine a holiday? Of course, ideas of comfort are individually determined. My husband prefers sitting on a straight-backed chair to watch television; I like succumbing to upholstery. And like so much else *having to do with habitation,* it is culturally determined. Think of the aristocratic Chinese women who slept on stone or ceramic pillows.

It is a cliché that people want to create the home as womb—even the implicit rhyme makes the connection. We don't want to be cold at home, and unless we are upper-class Brits of a certain masochistic historical moment, we want hot baths and showers. We have no memory as a species of how rare this is. "Nearly all of human life," Simone Weil says, "has always passed far from hot baths."[25] The old thinking of retiring to Florida or someplace where the temperature never dips; it is the rare senior who considers moving north. When I visit relatives in Florida, I am always amazed to consider that half of the year they are in the grips of hurricane threats. This, apparently, is more tolerable to them than the prospect of deep, long-lasting snows.

And perhaps the best way to understand what it is we mean by comfort is to examine the implications of its opposite. The opposite of comfort, it would seem to me, would fall under the categories of difficulty, and strain. The nineteenth-century poet W.B. Yeats wrote something called "The Fascination of What's Difficult," but most of us would not resonate to Yeats's variations on this theme. Ellen Richards, an early writer on "home economics," said, "The house as a home is merely outer clothing, which should fit as an overcoat should, without wrinkles and creases that show their ready-made character."[26]

Inhabiting a radical position on the spectrum of ideas of comfort, the French architect Le Corbusier tried to make a house that was built along modern lines, in which efficiency and convenience trumped the idea of comfort, which he considered a concern of weaklings. "The house," he said, "is a machine for living in. . . . One can be proud," he added, "of having a home as serviceable as a typewriter."[27]

Poor Le Corbusier: He couldn't have imagined a time when our younger citizens might find a typewriter as difficult to visualize as an astrolabe. But did anyone ever want to cuddle up with a typewriter? Did anybody ever hike scores of miles in the snow to get to a typewriter or dream of a typewriter when he or she was far from it, convinced that no other typewriter would be quite as provident of peace and restoration and delight? Are there any songs to a typewriter? The idea of home has been the inspiration for almost as many songs as the idea of romantic home: "The Hills of Home," "My Blue Heaven," "I'll Be Home for Christmas" . . . to name just a few. Even Crosby, Stills and Nash weighed in on the relatively property-unconscious late sixties; and Lucinda Williams did her own version of the girl rock singer's dream in the late nineties.

Architectural historian Robert Kerr draws the distinction between comfort and convenience. "Comfort," he says, "had to do with the passive enjoyment of the home by its owners, convenience had to do with the proper functioning of the house."[28] It is only within the last century that the idea of comfort and the idea of convenience became so closely wedded. This was because of the new reality of middle-class people regularly living without domestic help. A way of living that we take for granted: a nuclear family living in a separate dwelling, the domestic work being done by the woman of the house, dates, as a commonplace, only to the beginning of the twentieth century. Early writers on domestic science, like Catherine Beecher, insisted upon the importance of efficiency and convenience in the interests of women. But it is only in the twentieth century, when technology provided the possibility of servantless living that the warnings that had been cried by Beecher and her lot became rallying cries for women who insisted that a happy family life meant a house that took her labor into consideration.

We give up an enormous amount for our ideal of convenience. We may be committing both ecological and political suicide by our dependence on appliances that ten years ago did not even exist but that now we imagine we couldn't live without. But the most common victim on the altar of convenience is beauty: The Spanish town in which I discovered the house cut in two by warring families is a clear example of this. When I first visited there, the house was situated in a collection of small, whitewashed houses, cheek by jowl on a steep hilly street. There were few doors; more popular by far were beaded curtains, in front of which toothless, black-clad grandmothers sat, knitting endlessly. It never occurred to me that as they aged it might be difficult for them to carry their daily groceries up the hilly roads, or to wash their clothes in water delivered to them irregularly, depending on weather conditions, on a washboard in the sink. On a recent visit, I saw the town disfigured by a series of high-rises. They were buildings designed for senior citizens, with all the modern conveniences. The old ladies were now working out on treadmills instead of knitting and carrying their groceries up the hill. Were they happier? They professed that they were grateful for their new situations. Was it only we tourists who mourned the old traditional houses, with their graceful, ancient lines? When the old ladies said they missed the old ways, would they go back if they could? Probably not. But the new buildings are a grief to the eye and a scar on the landscape. How to measure that against the aching muscles, the chapped hands of the old ladies, formerly in black, now in leisure suits—healthier and longer lived by a decade than their mothers and grandmothers.

Sometimes a desire for beauty trumps a love of convenience. I perfectly well understand that Barcaloungers are very comfortable, may even be good for the back, may even put the body in an ideal posture for reading and listening to music. But I would rather have a fork in my eye than have a Barcalounger in my living room. And so I have a living room without a Barcalounger, but people don't walk into my house and say, "I see you don't have a Barcalounger here." The occasional standoff against convenience tends to be unmarked. Unless there is a dramatic contrast—a lovely old house standing stubbornly, resolutely in a sea of concrete high-risers—we see merely a lovely house, not an emblem of resistance. I return once again to my Spanish town. An old Dutch woman who lives in an orange grove refused to sell her house to developers. She endures bulldozing, the noise of workmen, the diminution of her light. But she will not leave, and as I write, she stays where she has been for forty years in her small, white, red tile house, pretending that the ugly monsters aren't breathing their foul breath through her kitchen windows, waiting with undisguised avidity for her death—which will allow them to bulldoze the house.

With her customary acuity, the French writer Colette speaks of a friend's radical choice against convenience. The friend, she says, "excels in

The idea of happiness has always
taken material form in the house,
whether cottage or castle;
it stands for permanence and
separation from the world.

—Simone de Beauvoir

imparting her strong personality to an apartment, and even a hotel room. Who is capable of overcoming the inertia of a *studio à confort*, of reviving a mezzanine as passive as an old horse . . . packed her bags and fled from a modern apartment which boasted . . . three very tall identical blocks of oppressive gray separated by courtyards. . . . She found words to reassure me and to convince herself. 'You see, I've constant hot water, and look how practical this bathroom is. And look at all these built in cupboards.' At the end of this display she left the place and was better off."[29]

But how do we know when we are better off? Why do I think I am better off without a Barcalounger, why did Colette's friend come to the conclusion that water and closet space weren't the answer to her prayers? Why do we make decisions that go against considerations of safety, convenience, and comfort? If we look to the habits of animals, they would seem to consider camouflage one of the most important elements in the construction of the home. Consider the sparrow, who covers her nest with lichens so that it will be all but invisible. But humans would seem to have more in common with the bowerbird, that avian outlier.

The male, called by some scientists as "the Avian Casanova," builds bowers that are decorated with feathers, butterfly wings, even car keys and pieces of blue glass. But these are bachelor pads, not places to raise the young. The sexually sated female goes somewhere much less glamorous to keep the kids in a safe neighborhood.

I am not, by any measure, a zoologist or animal behaviorist, but it seems to me that humans are the only creatures who want to combine security and display. We want to be safe, and we want to be seen. Moreover, we want to have visual access to the things that are a source of pride and pleasure to our eye. So our abodes are the lodging of our collections, our precious treasures: what we have held onto throughout time, what we want to look at on a regular basis, what we want people coming in from the outside to see that we treasure, and perhaps, more important, own.

But the relationship of the things we own to the space around them is a complex one. One person's cozy is another person's clutter. The late Victorians liked tables covered with bibelots, every surface embellished, nothing left bare. Compare that to a Japanese house, in which beauty is related to large areas of emptiness. As with cleanliness, there is no absolute good in taste. For a collector like Mario Praz, a home is importantly a place to house his collection. For Thoreau, almost anything is too much. He says, in *Walden*:

> *I had three pieces of limestone on my desk,*
> *but I was terrified to find that they required*
> *to be dusted daily, when the furniture of my*
> *mind was all undusted still, and I threw them*
> *out the window in disgust. How, then, could I*
> *have furnished a house?*[30]

Why is it that some houses, seen from the outside, strike one with a particular sense of rightness, and some cause a profound recoil in us, as if we were witness to a particularly public form of impropriety that bordered on the indecent? An experience of mine as quite a young child leads me to think that these responses go very deep. When I was five years old, I had to pass a house on my way to tap dance lessons that made me literally physically ill. It was a stucco house that had been painted a horrifying pink, the color of a Hostess Sno Ball. I would make my mother pull over to the side of the road so that I could vomit. Eventually, she became suspicious that the cause of my malaise was psychological rather than physical. She had no patience with my tearful outburst, "That house is making me sick. Because it is wrong."

That kind of literally visceral certainty may be understandable in a five-year-old, but it is a habit that a mature and flexible sensibility is better ridding itself from. Because we must often endure the wrongness of a house: a nouveau Tara on the former site of a fisherman's cottage, a McMansion too large for its own grounds, that dwarfs its neighbors and sticks out of the landscape like a cold sore on a rosebud mouth. The words that most frequently come to the mind of anyone who speaks about the fitness of the way we live are oddly classical: harmony. Balance.

In her 1910 work *The Decoration of Houses,* Edith Wharton says: "Good architecture and good decoration . . . must be based on rhythm and logic."[31] She criticizes what she sees as the particularly American failure of ostentatious bad taste in similarly classical terms: "The worst defects of furniture now made in America are due to an Athenian thirst for novelty, not always regulated by an Athenian sense of fitness."[32]

But how difficult to define and to apply all these words: rhythm, logic, fitness. There is no machine to measure or calibrate them, no authority—judicial, ecclesiastical—to give the final word. The architectural historian John Barrington Bailey posits the idea that divine visitation is the sign of a harmonious household: "Here is the *douceur de vivre* of the calm, well ordered house, the life of *juste milieu* where delicious meals are served on time and no guests stays too long . . . where there are suitable rooms for different hours and occupations. . . . The household gods delight in being here."[33] But most of us have not been gifted by a divine drop-in, nor have we found our Lares and Penates available to answer our questions: How much is too much? How many ornamental bronzes constitute excess? How much space is an experience not of emptiness, but of inhuman coldness? Too little can be a problem, too; Gaston Bachelard notes that "too much space smothers us much more than if there were not enough."[34] How do we know when we are building a place not for living in, but for making a point about or own importance? How do we know whether we are honoring tradition, or are victims of the chokehold of a dead past?

Speaking of Edith Wharton's taste, her friend, the aforementioned John Barrington Bailey, spoke of "Mrs. Wharton's complex feeling that our art and architecture should not merely consist of acquisitions and possessions, but be a reflection of the quality of our life and aspirations—what we ask of us and are willing to live by and live up to."[35]

Once again, we see the error of introducing ethical considerations into questions of habitation. I have known perfectly splendid human beings, whose lives were a joy and an enrichment to the larger world and to everyone they touched, who were happy to be living with their lava lamps from 1970 and were thrilled to show me their fourth bathroom wallpapered in what seemed to me a vision of Reynolds Wrap on amphetamines. And I have been in houses that were a hymn to harmony, proportion, a proper relation between emptiness and mass, between light and gravity—and have longed only to escape, so gloomy was the perfect air.

But most of us want the places we live to say something about us. To make the point that we are successful, desirable, intelligent, powerful, discriminating, and in the most extreme cases, worthy to be obeyed and feared. And yet we ask this of the places where we eat and sleep and bathe and raise our children. Like the bowerbird, we festoon our dwellings with blue glass and butterfly wings; like the sensible sparrow, we cover ourselves with lichens, for fear of the envious eyes of the predator. Which we define as: everybody in the world who doesn't live with us. What do we give up for houses who tell the world who we want to be? What are such statements worth? If the question "Where do you live?" is not as simple as it sounds, how about this one: "What's your house worth?"

So often I am struck by the strange habit familiar words have of turning incomprehensible when you look at them closely, using a sharp zoom lens. I confuse myself when I try to clarify what I mean when I say "worth." When I consult the dictionary, I find that the term is, for Merriam-Webster, as slippery as it is for me. They offer the following: "sufficiently good, important or interesting to justify a specified action; deserving to be treated or regarded as important; the value equivalent to that of someone or something under consideration, the level at which someone or something deserves to be valued."

The dictionary definition suggests that worth is always relative: something is worth as much, more, or less, than something else. But where is the fixed, unmoving term that we can think of as a stable basis for comparison?

I posed this question to a billionaire financier, a cultivated, intelligent, and humorous man to whom I happened to be seated beside at dinner. I approached him as a writer. I said that one of the clichés about someone's financial acuteness, or lack thereof, was, "He knows (or doesn't know) the value of a dollar." What I asked him was the value of a dollar. Since we no longer have a gold standard, I asked him (passing the butter, asking for the salt) what was the standard against which a dollar's worth is gauged. My charming companion laughed. "That's the question no one is supposed to ask," he said. "A dollar is worth whatever we all agree it's worth." "So," I said to him (pouring for the two of us another glass of exceptional Syrah), "you and I are in the same business. We both make stuff up. But my business is called fiction. Yours is called finance." We clinked glasses: coconspirators in the game of narrative creation.

But if high finance seems like a product of cloud-cuckoo-land to me, what about the housing market? How can it possibly be that the very same

A man travels the world over
in search of what he needs
and returns home to find it.

—George Moore

house on a piece of land that has been untouched by earthquake, flood, or plague of locusts be worth a million dollars in February, and a hundred thousand in November? What happened, I want to ask, and when people say things to me like "supply and demand," I say: Well, there weren't suddenly fewer people or more houses. It just seemed, one day, that the houses were worth less, that they had become suddenly undesirable, as if one turned to one's partner in bed and was struck by the question, "Why am I here?"

Given my training and habits of mind, I look for words whose source is religious, literary, or ethical to help me get a grip. To begin with, it would seem that questions of worth involve questions of sacrifice. What is to be given up for the desired quantity? This was made very clear to me when I had to decide that the Cape house I yearned for was not "worth" the time taken away from the kind of writing I wanted to do in order to produce writing that would generate more cash. I didn't want the pressure, the anxiety of debt. But the current economic debacle indicates that many people didn't agree with me. Perhaps they had a higher toleration for anxiety. Or perhaps debt wasn't real to them. This might have been a problem of their education. Brought up on Dickens, I could all too easily imagine myself and my family imprisoned, the children set to work in a blacking factory, all possibilities of a happy life cut off because of my profligacy. Many of my fellow Americans, it seems, didn't have those images in their brain. They thought their houses were "worth" the risk. As it turns out, the "value" of the houses was false, smaller than what was thought, the risk greater. If only they'd read Dickens! And they say literature has no relevance to real life! How much more useful to use a word like "greed"—which we find more in theology and poetry and novels than in economic texts—than a term like "subprime," or its near cousin, "bundling."

If I am confused by the definition of "worth" and the motivation of Americans (bankers and their clients) to take what seem to me ridiculous risks, I am equally baffled trying to understand why Americans are spending so much greater a proportion of their income on housing than ever before. According to U.S. Census Bureau Statistics, in 1950 the average American spent less than 18 percent of his or her annual income on housing; now the average is closer to 30 percent.

And yet, during the same period that housing costs were rising, the percentage of Americans owning their own homes was also climbing. The Census Bureau informs us that "in 2000, 2 in 3 householders in the United States owned their own home; in 1900 less than half owned their houses." Why do we put up with this? Is the strength of this American determination to own a home simply economic in its motivation? The idea being that only chumps rent, that at the end of the day you have nothing to show for the money you gave to a stranger (your landlord, always your enemy) every month. And nothing to leave to your children.

It is interesting that the drama of homeowning increases steadily as the reality that we will pass the home on to our children or heirs is diminishing. As we become a more mobile society, the old expectation that you would grow up and die in the place you were planted becomes less and less likely of fulfillment. As many of us approach old age, we think not of keeping the old homestead in the family, but find ourselves using yet another term we hadn't thought of when the Beach Boys were still boys: downsizing. The house that was the vessel for many of our young dreams begins to seem a burden; we still want a nest but as we find our wingspan diminished, we seem to crave a smaller one. And many of us know that we will have to contemplate a time in a place with another name that is new in the brain and on the tongue: assisted living. So the old dream of nuclear family independence, the two-or-more-story white house with the red roof and the picket fence gives way to preregistration in something that might easily be called Sunset Acres or Leisure Village.

As family structures attenuate, we have to rethink our reluctance to live communally. This might, for the planet and our psyches, not be such a bad thing. But we tend to see it as a diminishment.

"Owning a home lies at the heart of the American dream." So declared President Bush in 2002, introducing his "Homeownership Challenge." It might be, at least, more truthful to acknowledge that the supposedly hardheaded decisions about wealth expenditure in relation to habitation are more the stuff of poetry than economics. Or at least we might need to consider that we need a new narrative to help us make sense of the way we live, and what is at stake in our decisions. What the way we live is "worth."

three

What Do We Mean by Home?

Home sweet home. A man's home is his castle. Home is where the heart is. Neighborhood, homeland, demesne, estate, plantation, ghetto, flat. *All these words signifying: the place of habitation. The place where we live.*

I am writing this from home. I know what I mean when I say that. I have left a place where it was meaningful to say, "I wasn't living where I lived." For a week I am in my New York apartment with the paintings I treasure, the dishes I have served so many loved people with, the bed that looks onto the treadmill which ruins the proportions of the room, but which makes me healthy and so happy. The first day I am home I have lunch with one friend, dinner with another. The second day I go to the Metropolitan Museum. The third, I see my dentist and my doctors. I travel on the subway. I walk to buy my groceries and the weight and strain of them fills me with joy. Then I travel to my house in the country. The last of the crocuses waited for me, the most enduring snowdrops. The first daffodils, the ones that grow in shelter, opened just, it seemed, to greet me. The dogs run free. I sit at my desk, write in my journal, observe the progress of my pignut hickory.

Do I deserve it?

Do any of us?

And how would we know?

Perhaps we must agree with Colette when she says: "Our ideal dwelling place always remains more or less imaginary."[36] And if this is the case, in our attempts at finding a satisfactory way to live, perhaps we should take the advice of another writer, Samuel Beckett, the poet laureate of the land of discomfort and displacement. With his

Home is not where you live,
but where they understand you.

—Christian Morgenstern

characteristic stoic courage he urges us: "Fail. Fail again. Fail better."

Or perhaps we should, like Dorothy Gale in *The Wizard of Oz,* click our ruby slippers together and repeat in our confused delirium: "There's no place like home . . . there's no place like home."

Endnotes

1   Gaston Bachelard, *The Poetics of Space* (Boston: Beacon Press, 1994), 213.

2   Paul Krugman, "Home Not-So-Sweet Home," *The New York Times,* June 23, 2008: www.nytimes.com/2008/06/23/opinion/23krugman.html.

3   Phillippe Ariès and Georges Duby, eds. *A History of Private Life*, vol. 3 (Cambridge: Belknap Press of Harvard University Press, 1987), 342.

4   Mario Praz, *An Illustrated History of Interior Decoration: From Pompeii to Art Nouveau* (New York: Thames and Hudson, 1982), 23.

5   Bachelard, 81.

6   Rebecca R. Kahlenberg, "Alarms Fortify Security Feeling," *Washington Post,* July 23, 2005: F01.

7   Ariès, 403.

8   Simon Schama, *The Embarrassment of Riches: An Interpretation of Dutch Culture in the Golden Age* (New York: Vintage, 1997), 389.

9   Schama, 570.

10 Praz, 26.

11 Witold Rybczynski, *Home* (New York: Viking Penguin, 1986), 34.

12 Ariès, 162.

13 Rybczynski, 43.

14 Mary Douglas, *Purity and Danger: An Analysis of Concepts of Pollution and Taboo* (London: Routledge Classics, 2002), 2.

15 Bachelard, 6.

16 W. H. Auden, *Selected Poems,* Edward Mendelson, ed. (New York: Vintage Books), 275.

17 Katherine Ashenburg, *The Dirt on Clean: An Unsanitized History* (New York: North Point Press, 2007), 263–5. Surprisingly, for a writer on cleanliness Ashenberg is quite sloppy in her footnotes. The writer on domestic economy isn't Harriet Beecher Stowe, the author of *Uncle Tom's Cabin,* it's her sister, Catherine Beecher.

18 Auden, 273.

19 Ibid., 285.

20 Ibid., 274.

21 Douglas, 2.

22 Ashenburg, 263–4.

23 Rybczynski, 26.

24 Ibid., 221.

25 Weil, *Intimations of Christianity Among the Ancient Greeks* (London: Routledge, 1998), 25.

26 Rybczynski, 160.

[27] Ibid., 190.

[28] Ibid., 160.

[29] Colette, *Places,* David Le Vay trans. (London: Peter Owen Ltd., 1970), 3.

[30] Praz, 21.

[31] Ogden Codman Jr. and Edith Wharton, *The Decoration of Houses* (New York: W.W. Norton, 1978), 10.

[32] Ibid., 27.

[33] Ibid., vii.

[34] Bachelard, 221.

[35] Codman and Wharton, xviii.

[36] Colette, 27.

About the Author

Mary Gordon is the author of seven novels, including *The Company of Women*, *Final Payments*, *Spending*, and the forthcoming *The Love of My Youth*; the memoirs *The Shadow Man* and *Circling My Mother;* and a collection of short stories. She is the recipient of a Lila Wallace–Reader's Digest Writers' Award, a Guggenheim Fellowship, and the 1997 O. Henry Award for best story. She teaches at Barnard College and lives in New York City.